PET
Practice Tests 2

Diana L. Fried-Booth and
Louise Hashemi

CAMBRIDGE
UNIVERSITY PRESS

Published by the Press Syndicate of the University of Cambridge
The Pitt Building, Trumpington Street, Cambridge CB2 1RP
40 West 20th Street, New York, NY 10011–4211, USA
10 Stamford Road, Oakleigh, Melbourne 3166, Australia

© Cambridge University Press 1991

First published 1991
Fourth printing 1994

Printed in Great Britain by
Scotprint Ltd., Musselburgh

ISBN 0 521 356806 Student's Book
ISBN 0 521 356814 Teacher's Book
ISBN 0 521 355907 Set of 2 cassettes

VN

Contents

Thanks   *iv*

Introduction to the student   *v*

Unit 1   Shopping and services   *1*

Unit 2   Health and medicine   *19*

Unit 3   Travel and tourism   *37*

Unit 4   Family, education and society   *55*

Unit 5   PET practice test paper   *71*

Visual material for the Oral: *colour section at centre of book*

Thanks

We should like to thank all the students and staff at the various schools where the material for *PET Practice Tests 2* was piloted who took the time and trouble to record their comments and reactions. Particular thanks also to the students and staff at The Chichester School of English who contributed towards producing 'sample' answers for the final version of the Teacher's Book. We are also indebted to Jeanne McCarten and Annie Cornford for their encouragement and support during the writing and revision of this material.

Acknowledgements

The authors and publishers are grateful to Rover Cars for kind permission to reproduce the photographs A, B and C on p. 79 and to Vauxhall Motors Ltd for kind permission to reproduce photograph D on p. 79.

Photographs by Abbas Hashemi on pp. 1, 2, 19, 20, 37, 38, 55, 56, 71 and 72; Jeremy Pembrey on pp. 13, 14, 32, 33, 49, 50, 51, 66, 68, 84 and 85.
Drawings by Abbas Hashemi on pp. 11 and 27; Mike Hingley on pp. 12, 16, 31, 32, 33, 70, 83, 84 and 85; Peter Joyce on pp. 23, 30, 49, 50 and 51; David Mostyn on pp. 13, 15, 45, 62, 66 and 67.

Colour oral section: photographs by Howard Fried-Booth (1B, 1C, 2A), Jeremy Pembrey (2B, 2C, 3B, 3C, 4C, 4D); artwork by Mike Hingley (3A) and David Mostyn (1A, 5B).

Introduction to the student

This book is for students who are preparing to take the Preliminary English Test (PET). It contains five units or practice tests. The first four are based on different topics: shopping and services; health and medicine; travel and tourism; family, education and society. These units will help you to learn and revise the vocabulary and structures which are covered in your coursebook. The last unit, which is like the 'real' PET, is *not* based on a particular topic. This unit can be used as a final practice test just before you take the examination.

If you work through this book it will help you to recognise the kinds of questions you will have to answer in the examination. There are four parts in each test: reading, writing, listening and speaking, although the oral section of the test is taken separately.

The book is meant to be used in class with a teacher but you can use it if you are working alone to practise the reading, writing and listening parts of the test.

If you are studying by yourself you will need the cassettes, which contain the recordings for the listening part of the test, and the Teacher's Book, which contains the answer Key for all the exercises and the tapescripts of the recordings. You will probably need extra help with the speaking part of the test, so ask a teacher or a native speaker to help you.

We hope that you will enjoy using the book (even if you don't finally take the examination). Good Luck!

Unit 1   Shopping and services

READING

QUESTION 1

Look at the five pictures of signs below. Someone asks you what each sign means. For each sign put a tick in one of the boxes – like this √ – to show the correct answer.

1

☐ Dogs must wait outside.

☐ Dogs must walk with their owners.

☐ Dogs must be kept on a chain.

☐ Dogs must be held.

2.

☐ Everything is cheaper this week.

☐ No extra charges next week.

☐ Usual prices this week.

☐ Cheaper prices next week.

3.

☐ You can send your groceries from here.

☐ You can store your groceries here.

☐ You can get your free groceries here.

☐ You can have your groceries sent to you.

4.

☐ Cleaning now costs twice as much.

☐ Cleaning costs are now cheaper.

☐ Cleaning costs are going up.

☐ Cleaning costs will stay the same.

5.

☐ We cannot deliver papers at the weekend.

☐ We plan to stop delivering papers five days from now.

☐ You must tell us five days early if you don't want papers.

☐ Please tell us if you don't want papers at the weekend.

QUESTION 2

Read the article below and circle the letter next to the word that best fits each space.

EXAMPLE: The shop .... gave me the wrong change.

  (A) assistant   B person   C people   D one

> C & A is probably one of the largest family fashion stores in the world, and their shops are a familiar sight in (1) .... High Streets in Britain. But many British people would be surprised to learn (2) .... this fashion company has Dutch origins. Founded in the small market town of Sneek in 1841, the first C & A shop (3) .... opened by two brothers called Clemens and August Brenninkmeyer. The initials of their first names formed the name of the shop. As trade grew, more (4) .... were opened across Europe and in 1922 C & A came to Britain. (5) .... success was immediate and the store was a major influence in bringing down the (6) .... of women's clothes. It was the two brothers (7) .... started the 5-day working week, at a time when shopkeepers in Britain expected their (8) .... to work a 6-day week. Today C & A employs many thousands of people. All the stores are attractively (9) .... with good use of space, lighting and plenty of individual changing rooms where (10) .... can try things on in comfort before they buy.

1.	A	every	B	most	C	more	D	each
2.	A	that	B	if	C	and	D	because
3.	A	were	B	have	C	had	D	was
4.	A	stores	B	places	C	parts	D	houses
5.	A	They	B	This	C	That	D	Their
6.	A	value	B	figures	C	cost	D	money
7.	A	which	B	who	C	what	D	whom
8.	A	staff	B	groups	C	officers	D	employers
9.	A	drawn	B	designed	C	set	D	put
10.	A	customers	B	patients	C	one	D	persons

QUESTION 3

Look at these advertisements which have been placed in a shop window in Mells, then answer the questions.

(A) FLAT TO RENT
Owner going abroad for 1 year would like to let Modern 2 bedroomed flat. Comfortably furnished. £200 per month.
Tel. 336587

(B) FLAT TO SHARE
Close to city centre
Would suit young person
Share bathroom and kitchen
£80 per week
Ring 61111 after 6 pm.

(C) MUSIC COURSES
Learn to play your favourite instrument from as little as £3 a lesson.
For more details write:
The Director
Music School
Cathedral Green, Mells

(D) GARDENER WANTED
Elderly lady requires help in garden 2 mornings a week from 9 - 12. Good pay.
Ring: 332050

(E) FISH
Enjoy watching these beautiful fish!
Large Fish bowl and gold-fish for sale. Will deliver.
Tel: 47205

(F) Looking for a job??
You can earn up to £100 a week delivering advertisements.
Evenings only from 6-10pm including Saturdays.
Contact: Mailshots
             Hollow St, Mells.

(G) Learning the Piano?
Piano - reasonable condition, would suit a beginner.
£100 o.n.o.
Ring 87161 any time

(H) "SHINING SHAPES"
Strong, careful person to help in glass store Mon-Fri 7.30am-2.30pm some Saturdays
Excellent rate of pay for steady worker.
For details Phone 27732

(I) MUSIC TEACHER
Recently retired. Fully trained with over 40 years' experience. Violin to all ages. Contact:
   Mrs Sterling
   1 The Close
   Mells

(J) HORSE RIDING LESSONS!
Learn to ride in 6 easy lessons. Small classes. Sunday mornings. Children especially welcome. Tel: 73466

The people below reply to one advertisement each. Write the most suitable letter A–J to show which advertisement you think they might choose.

1. Peter is out of work and needs a job; his wife has an evening job while he looks after the children. ☐

2. Wendy has taken a job in Mells and is looking for her own independent accommodation. ☐

3. Ruth is hoping to get married and although she already works full-time from 9 a.m.–5 p.m. she is looking for a way to earn some extra money. ☐

4. Rosemary's aunt has given her a piano; she can't play it but she is interested in learning. ☐

5. Matthew wants his parents to buy him a pet for his tenth birthday, but they live in a small flat without a garden. ☐

QUESTION 4

Look at the page from the Manchester shopping guide. If you think a statement is true, put a tick in the box under 'Yes'. If not, tick the box under 'No'.

		Yes	No
1.	This leaflet describes a new shopping area just outside Manchester.	☐	☐
2.	You can reach Market Street by going along Deansgate.	☐	☐
3.	The Market Centre is built below ground.	☐	☐
4.	King Street has a large fruit market.	☐	☐
5.	The pavement café in St Ann's Square has just been opened.	☐	☐
6.	The Royal Exchange Shopping Centre is inside an old building.	☐	☐
7.	The Arndale Centre is built on three floors.	☐	☐
8.	The High Street Market is in the square next to the Arndale Centre.	☐	☐
9.	There are more than 200 stalls in the High Street Market.	☐	☐
10.	You can park your car in the Arndale Centre.	☐	☐

"If you're looking for the best shopping choice in the North West, then City Centre Manchester is the right place."

Whatever you are shopping for, you'll almost certainly find it in City Centre Manchester. You'll find more choice and your shopping will be more enjoyable in City Centre Manchester – where you're right in the heart of things.

"Let's start with one of the main shopping thoroughfares in the City – Market Street."

Market Street has now been pedestrianised and runs from Piccadilly Gardens down to the road known as Deansgate. Here, you'll find many famous top-name department stores, chain stores and a host of other shops, offering everything from the latest fashions and the tops of the pops, to household goods, holidays abroad and somewhere to eat. While you're in the area, don't miss the Market Centre, a large underground market in Spring Gardens, off Market Street.

"Manchester's most exclusive shopping areas."

King Street, St. Ann's Square and Deansgate. Here you'll find unusual shops, both large and small, including leading fashion houses, jewellers, booksellers and shops selling traditional and modern furnishings, plus another of Manchester's top department stores. St. Ann's Square has now been tastefully pedestrianised, complementing the quality shops. A pavement cafe is a new feature.
The Royal Exchange Shopping Centre, between St. Ann's Square and Cross Street, is housed in the historic Royal Exchange Building next to the Royal Exchange Theatre. It is a fascinating centre for exclusive fashions, arts, crafts and specialist shops selling top quality merchandise

"The Arndale Centre – probably the largest covered shopping area in Europe."

The Arndale Centre has to be seen to be believed. Wide, air-conditioned boulevards on two levels lead you in comfort around the major stores and 200 smaller shops and eating places, whatever the weather. You'll also find the High Street Market within the Arndale Centre. This covered market has nearly 200 stalls offering foods and a complete range of goods at bargain prices. The Arndale Centre is easy to get to, with parking for 1,800 cars, and an adjoining bus station.
Chinatown. Situated between Piccadilly and Princess Street. Chinatown offers a wealth of Chinese restaurants, speciality supermarkets and gift shops.

QUESTION 5

Read this passage and then answer the questions below. You must put a tick in the correct box or write in a few words.

Charlotte Tocher made a once-in-a-lifetime visit to China last October and took lots of photographs. When she got back she decided to send away her films for printing one at a time. In this way she would more easily be able to match her photographs to the diary she had kept while she was there. It was a good thing that she did, because the first film she sent to the company for printing was lost.

Miss Tocher was very upset that she would never see her precious pictures of Shanghai and Souzhou. The company offered her a free roll of film, but Miss Tocher refused to accept this offer and wrote back to say that their offer wasn't enough. They then offered her £20 but she refused this too and asked for £75, which she thought was quite fair. When the firm refused to pay she said she would go to court. Before the matter went to court, however, the firm decided to pay Miss Tocher £75. This shows what can be done if you make the effort to complain to a firm or manufacturer and insist on getting fair treatment.

1. This is from ☐ a guidebook.

    ☐ a letter.

    ☐ a magazine.

    ☐ a diary.

2. What is the writer trying to do? ☐ to complain about photographic printing

    ☐ to give advice on how to complain

    ☐ to warn us about going to court

    ☐ to inform us about legal problems

3. Why was it a good thing that Miss Tocher sent her films away one at a time?

    ....

    ....

4. When Miss Tocher said she would go to court the company thought ....

....

....

5. Look at the following letters. Show which one you think was the LAST one Miss Tocher received from the film company by circling the letter A, B, C or D.

A

Acme *film processing*

Unit 6,
Richmond Lane
Ringway Industrial Estate
Readham
Bucks

our ref JB/JJ/29
your ref

Dear Miss Tocher,
We apologise for the loss of your film and understand how upset you were. We should like you to accept a cheque for £20 towards the purchase of extra rolls of film . . .

B

Acme *film processing*

Unit 6,
Richmond Lane
Ringway Industrial Estate
Readham
Bucks

our ref JB/JJ/29
your ref

Dear Miss Tocher,
As a result of the court judgement we are sending you a cheque for £75. Please accept our apologies for the loss of your film. Assuring you of our best attention in future . . .

C

Acme *film processing*

Unit 6,
Richmond Lane
Ringway Industrial Estate
Readham
Bucks

our ref JB/JJ/29
your ref

Dear Miss Tocher,
Thank you for your latest letter. You will be pleased to know that the company has decided to send you a cheque for £75.
Please see attached . . .

D

Acme *film processing*

Unit 6,
Richmond Lane
Ringway Industrial Estate
Readham
Bucks

our ref JB/JJ/29
your ref

Dear Miss Tocher,
We are writing to inform you of the decision reached by our company. We have decided to send you a cheque for £20 together with 2 free rolls of film which you will receive shortly. We hope you find this satisfactory . . .

WRITING

QUESTION 6

Here are some sentences about shopping. Finish the second sentence so that it has the same meaning as the first.

EXAMPLE: Sandra prefers supermarkets to small shops.

        Sandra thinks supermarkets *are better than small shops.*

1. 'Have you got a pale blue sweater?' I asked the shop assistant.

   I asked ....

2. She showed me one that was too small.

   The one she ....

3. 'How much is the red sweater?' I asked.

   'How much does ....

4. The red one was more expensive than the blue one.

   The blue sweater ....

5. So I bought neither!

   So I didn't..

QUESTION 7

You want to join a postal shopping plan. Fill in the form below.

SHOPPING BY POST

Join this special club for the best clothes at affordable prices.
Just fill in this form and post it today!

1   MR   MRS   MS

2   SURNAME ....

3   INITIALS ....

4   ADDRESS ....

     ....

     ....

5   PHONE NO ....

6   AGE ....

7   DO YOU HAVE A BANK ACCOUNT?   **YES/NO**

7a NAME OF BANK ....

8   ARE YOU A STUDENT?   **YES/NO**

8a NAME OF SCHOOL OR COLLEGE ....

9   ARE YOU EMPLOYED?   **YES/NO**

9a NAME OF COMPANY ....

10 WHAT SORT OF CLOTHES DO YOU LIKE TO WEAR?

     ....

     ....

     ....

     ....

     ....

11 DO YOU HAVE ANY SPECIAL NEEDS?

     (eg unusual size, for sport, dancing, holiday etc)

     ....

     ....

     ....

     ....

     ....

QUESTION 8

A friend of yours has got a new job in Ingsdon, and wants to know something about the town where he/she is now going to live. Use the information on the map below to write a letter telling him/her what to expect. The letter has been started for you. Use about 100 words.

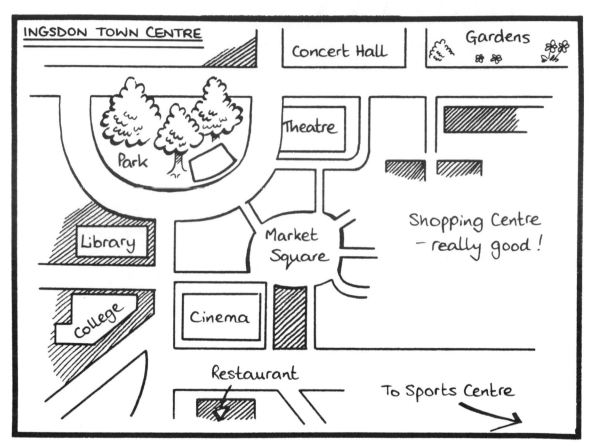

Dear ....

I think you will be interested to know what Ingsdon is like ....

....

....

....

....

....

LISTENING

QUESTION 9

Put a tick in the box you think is the most suitable.

EXAMPLE:

☐   ☐   ☐   ☑

1.

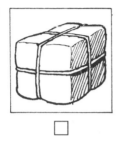   

☐   ☐

☐   ☐

2.

☐   ☐   ☐   ☐

⟫→

3.

4.

5.

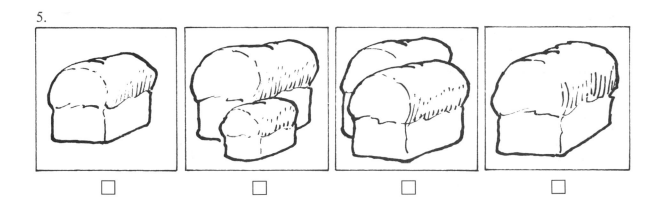

6.

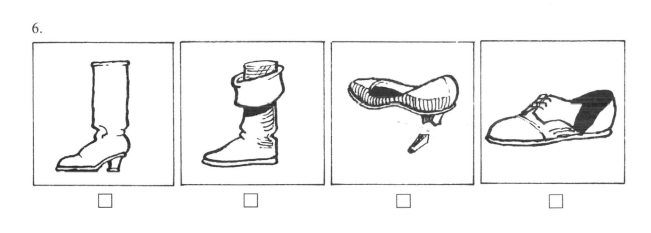

7.

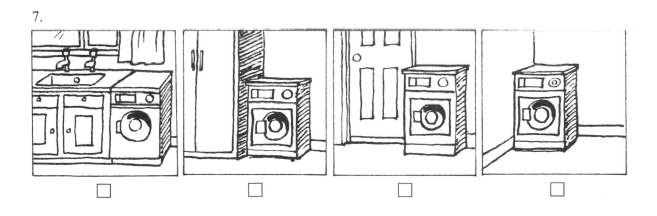

QUESTION 10

Look at the plan of Brimston and put a tick in the box you think is the most suitable.

BRIMSTON CITY CENTRE

Bus Station

① Barrs' sell
gloves. ☐
boots. ☐
shoes. ☐
socks. ☐

② Crampling & Co sell
hand-made cloth. ☐
women's clothes. ☐
foreign fashions. ☐
cheap clothes. ☐

③ Greens' sell
old love stories. ☐
children's stories. ☐
old books. ☐
expensive books. ☐

④ Garretts' sell
travellers' cheques. ☐
football boots. ☐
raincoats. ☐
sports clothing. ☐

TEA SHOP | TRAVEL AGENCY

⑤ Brimston Craft Centre sells
cakes. ☐
sweets. ☐
dresses. ☐
toys. ☐

⑥ Drovers' sell
pictures of animals. ☐
wrapping paper. ☐
cheese. ☐
perfume. ☐

QUESTION 11

Write in the information needed below.

Things to buy:
_____

Weekend hill walking –

    essential clothing: strong ① _____
                      ② _____ pairs of socks
                      ③ _____ and jacket
                            (waterproof if possible)
                cotton ④ _____
                two ⑤ _____
                    ⑥ _____ and gloves (perhaps)

Deep-sea diving –

    essential clothing: ⑦ _____ swimsuits
                plenty of large ⑧ _____
                2 pairs of ⑨ _____
                1 pair of sandals
                1 cotton jumper
                lightweight ⑩ _____

QUESTION 12

If you agree with the statement put a tick under 'Yes'. If you do not agree, put a tick under 'No'.

		Yes	*No*
1.	They want to buy Stephanie a present for her birthday.	☐	☐
2.	The wife believes Stephanie would like a book.	☐	☐
3.	The husband wants to give Stephanie a saucepan.	☐	☐
4.	The wife thinks that Stephanie would like the soap.	☐	☐
5.	The wife is too busy to buy the present.	☐	☐
6.	The husband is worried about choosing the present.	☐	☐

Unit 2   Health and medicine

READING

QUESTION 1

Look at the five pictures of signs below. Someone asks you what each sign means. For each sign put a tick in one of the boxes — like this √ — to show the correct answer.

1.

☐ Your dentist may give you medicine.

☐ You have to bring your medicine with you.

☐ Ask your dentist if you need some medicine.

☐ Your dentist needs to know about your medicine.

2.

☐ Take two tablets a day.

☐ Take three tablets a day.

☐ Take five tablets a day.

☐ Take six tablets a day.

⫸→

3

CIGARETTES CAN SERIOUSLY DAMAGE YOUR HEALTH

☐ These cigarettes are safer than ordinary ones.

☐ You are not allowed to smoke here.

☐ Smoking annoys other people.

☐ People who smoke may get ill.

4.

THIS HOSPITAL HAS NO EMERGENCY DEPARTMENT

☐ Accident patients are not admitted here.

☐ The emergency department is closed.

☐ This hospital only accepts accident patients.

☐ Contact this hospital in an emergency.

5.

HOME VISITS: YOUR DOCTOR'S TIME IS VALUABLE. PLEASE DO NOT CALL HIM/HER OUT UNLESS REALLY NECESSARY.

☐ You will have to pay if the doctor visits your home.

☐ The doctor will visit you in hospital if necessary.

☐ You can call the doctor out if you are seriously ill.

☐ The doctor can only visit you during the day.

QUESTION 2

Read the article below and circle the letter next to the word that best fits each space.

EXAMPLE: She .... the nurse for another blanket.

   A said   B requested   Ⓒ asked   D spoke

Advice for travellers who may fall ill while abroad
Most British people go abroad on holiday, to visit
family, or on short business trips. People are
(1) .... to find out how to get urgent treatment
before leaving the UK. They have to (2) .... a form
which explains what they (3) .... do if they fall ill
or (4) .... an accident, and what arrangements
exist in (5) .... country for medical treatment. The
regulations are fairly simple but (6) .... people do
not have this information, they may (7) .... that
private medical care is extremely expensive. It is not
unusual for people to discover that they do not have
(8) .... money with them to (9) .... the total
costs and (10) .... such circumstances an already
difficult situation becomes even more complicated.

1.	A	advised	B	suggested	C	said	D	spoken
2.	A	put	B	bring	C	fill	D	get
3.	A	ought	B	will	C	should	D	may
4.	A	have	B	get	C	happen	D	take
5.	A	their	B	each	C	one	D	this
6.	A	because	B	whether	C	as	D	if
7.	A	look	B	want	C	find	D	know
8.	A	enough	B	little	C	few	D	full
9.	A	pay	B	give	C	spend	D	have
10.	A	on	B	in	C	at	D	up

QUESTION 3

Here is part of a guide to ways of using plants as medicine. Read the information about the plants, then answer the questions.

PLANTS FOR HEALTH

Chamomile

This is an old and valuable medicine for a number of aches and pains. It can be taken as a drink to help when one is suffering earache or toothache, or if one has stomach pains.

Greater Celandine

Chewing the root of this plant may help reduce the pain of toothache and the juice is used to clear the eyes. Patients should be careful not to drink too much of the juice as this can be bad for the stomach.

Comfrey

This plant has long been recognized as being very helpful in mending broken bones. A drink made from the root of the plant can be very helpful to anyone who is troubled with a cough.

Ribwort

For cuts, the fresh leaves can be prepared and used to stop bleeding. It can also be made into a drink with honey, to help when there is difficulty with breathing.

Rosemary

This plant, well-known in cooking, and also often used to make the hair shine after washing, is very good for headaches when dried and used as a tea.

Elderflower

Elderflower water is frequently used to keep the skin clear and fresh. The berries can be made into an excellent hot drink, which is very pleasant if one is suffering from a cold.

Look at the pictures below and write the most suitable letter A–F to show which plant you think might help each patient. More than one answer may be possible.

1. ☐ 2. ☐ 3. ☐

4. ☐ 5. ☐ 6. ☐

QUESTION 4

Look at the newspaper article about a hospital and decide whether the following statements are true. If you think a statement is true, put a tick in the box under 'Yes'. If not, tick the box under 'No'.

		Yes	*No*
1.	The local hospital was nearly closed ten years ago.	☐	☐
2.	The government has had to spend a lot of money to repair the local hospital.	☐	☐
3.	Old people will find it hard to go to the city hospital.	☐	☐
4.	Working people think the local hospital is unnecessary.	☐	☐
5.	Local people prefer to nurse dying relatives in their own homes.	☐	☐
6.	The nurses at the local hospital make difficulties for patients' families.	☐	☐
7.	Some specialists visit the local hospital regularly.	☐	☐
8.	Dr Chan believes it would be better to see all the patients at the city hospital.	☐	☐

Hospital to close

Shock announcement

The Regional Health Department has announced that the local hospital will be closed in two years time.

Local area

The hospital was built in 1935 to serve this small town and the villages and farms in the area. Ten years ago the Regional Health Department suggested closing the hospital, but local people fought the idea so hard that the hospital was allowed to stay open.

Money

Since then a lot of money has been given by people who use the hospital in order to keep the building and equipment in good condition.

Patients speak out

Our reporter asked a number of patients what they felt:

"It's particularly important for us older people who live in the villages. We haven't got cars to drive all the way to the city hospital to see a specialist – it's fifty miles – you can't get there and back on the bus in one day."

"Look, I've got a car so I can get to the city and back. The problem is that I'm going to lose a day's wages while I do it. The local hospital may be small, but it's here, and I can be in and out in an hour."

Family feelings

"When my grandmother was dying, she was very ill for a long time. We could visit her every day because she was near us. The nurses were wonderfully kind, they're all part of a small team, so they knew all the family and were very helpful to us. It was a bad time, but if the hospital wasn't there, we wouldn't have had the equipment to nurse her at home, so she'd have been far away, not seeing us often, that would have been much worse."

Top specialists

It is said that it is not possible for top specialists to work at such a small hospital, but in fact there are specialists who come to the hospital every week. When asked about the cost of this, Dr A. Chan told our reporter, "It saves time and money for one specialist to travel 100 miles instead of asking 20 patients to travel the same distance to see the specialist in the city . . ."

QUESTION 5

Read this passage and then answer the questions below. You must put a tick in the correct box or write in a few words.

Along with jogging and swimming, cycling is one of the best all-round forms of exercise. It can help to increase your strength and energy, giving you more efficient muscles and a stronger heart. But increasing your strength is not the only advantage of cycling. Because you're not carrying the weight of your body on your feet, it's a good form of exercise for people with painful feet or backs. However, with all forms of exercise it's important to start slowly and build up gently. Doing too much too quickly can damage muscles that aren't used to working. If you have any doubts about taking up cycling for health reasons, talk to your doctor and ask his/her advice.

Ideally you should be cycling at least two or three times a week. For the exercise to be doing you good, you should get a little out of breath. Don't worry that if you begin to lose your breath, it could be dangerous and there must be something wrong with your heart. This is simply not true; shortness of breath shows that the exercise is having the right effect. However, if you find you are in pain then you should stop and take a rest.

1. This piece of writing is for ☐ children.

   ☐ doctors.

   ☐ anyone.

   ☐ sportsmen and women.

2. What is the writer's purpose? ☐ to amuse

   ☐ to worry

   ☐ to persuade

   ☐ to warn

3. People with back problems might go cycling because

   ....

   ....

4. What is the disadvantage of sudden exercise?

  ....

  ....

5. Which of these notices has the same ideas as the writer? Put a tick in the box next to the correct one.

LATE FOR WORK?

Do you get held up in traffic on the way to work? Do they always cancel the train you were going to catch? If so, we have the answer for you. Buy a bike! You'll be in control, keep your boss happy and be healthier too.

A ☐

ARE YOU ALWAYS TIRED?

What you need is a bicycle! Go cycling regularly and you'll soon be able to feel that extra energy. It may be difficult at first but keep it up and you'll get stronger and healthier too. If you have any medical problems, check with your doctor first.

C ☐

CYCLING FOR PLEASURE

An excellent form of exercise, cycling allows you to see the country and improve your health at the same time. Why not join your local cycle touring club today?

D ☐

A BIKE RIDE A DAY KEEPS THE DOCTOR AWAY

Cycling: one of the safest forms of exercise there is. A daily bike ride will help improve your breathing (especially if you smoke) and gently exercise your muscles. Hurry along to your local bike shop now and find out all you need to know.

B ☐

WRITING

QUESTION 6

Here are some sentences about a medical problem. Finish the second sentence so that it has the same meaning as the first.

EXAMPLE: He had a weak heart which meant he couldn't walk very far.

His *heart was so weak he couldn't walk very far.*

1. John was too ill to go to work.

   John was not ....

2. He was examined by his doctor.

   His doctor ....

3. The doctor told him he worked too hard.

   'You ....

4. 'I advise you to take a holiday,' the doctor continued.

   'You'd ....

5. 'If you don't rest you really will be ill!'

   'Unless ....

QUESTION 7

You have been on holiday in a foreign country and have had an accident. Fill in the insurance form below.

SUNSPOT HOLIDAYS
INSURANCE CLAIM FORM

full name .... MR/MRS/MISS/MS

address ....

....

....

date of birth ....

occupation ....

Where did the accident happen? Please give the exact place.

....

....

....

Describe how you were hurt as clearly as possible please.

....

....

....

How long did you spend in hospital?

....

SIGNED ....

DATE ....

QUESTION 8

Your doctor has advised you to change your eating habits in order to improve your health. Below is the paper your doctor has given you. Write a letter to your friend explaining in general what you have to do and giving your opinion of it. Use about 100 words.

The Springfield easy-to-follow healthy eating plan for a fitter fresher you!

As much as you like.

Any two of these each day.

A *little* of these.

Not at all!

Dear ....,

Thanks for the postcard. I'm glad everything's well with you. I myself am feeling

LISTENING

QUESTION 9

Put a tick in the box you think is the most suitable.

EXAMPLE:

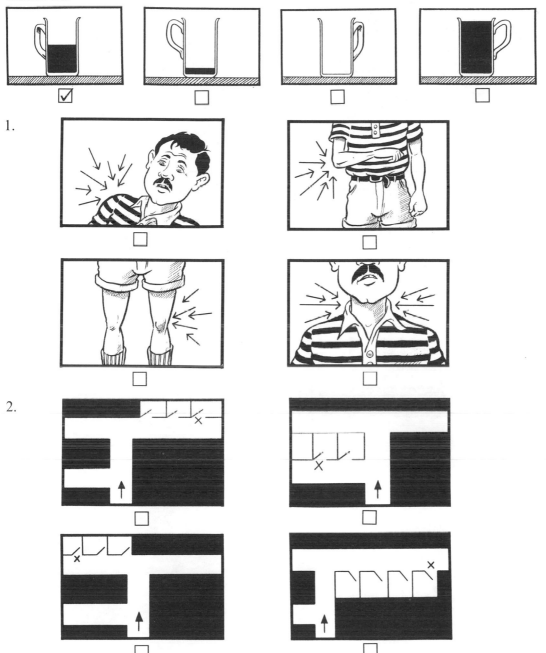

3.

☐   ☐

☐   ☐

4.

☐   ☐   ☐   ☐

5.

☐   ☐

☐   ☐

6.

7.

QUESTION 10

You are spending a weekend at Greenaways Health Farm. Here are some notes about what you are going to do. Put a tick in the box you think is the most suitable.

GREENWAYS
HEALTH FARM

1. After this talk we'll have tea. ☐
   coffee. ☐
   fruit juice. ☐
   a light meal. ☐

2. At 6 p.m. there's a talk about losing weight. ☐
   eating the right food. ☐
   cookery. ☐
   finding good restaurants. ☐

3. Supper is at 6.45. ☐
   7.15. ☐
   7.40. ☐
   7.45. ☐

4. The film is about walking. ☐
   gardening. ☐
   books. ☐
   medicines. ☐

5. There's a class about exercise plans tomorrow before breakfast. ☐
   before lunch. ☐
   after lunch. ☐
   after tea. ☐

6. The cookery class is in the workroom. ☐
   Room 4. ☐
   the kitchen. ☐
   the dining room. ☐

QUESTION 11

Write in the information needed below.

Barrington Regional Hospital
accident in-patient admission card

MR/MRS/MISS/MS

1 surname _____

2 initials _____

3 date of birth **DAY**_____ **MONTH**_____ **YEAR**_____

4 address _____

_____

_____

5 description of injury _____

_____

_____

6 cause of injury _____

_____

_____

QUESTION 12

If you agree with the statement put a tick in the box under 'Yes'. If you do not agree, put a tick under 'No'.

		Yes	No
1.	The woman is complaining.	☐	☐
2.	It's three weeks since the doctor saw this patient.	☐	☐
3.	The woman took the doctor's advice.	☐	☐
4.	The woman has given up sugar and salt.	☐	☐
5.	The doctor thinks the patient needs a new drug.	☐	☐
6.	The woman is satisfied with the doctor's suggestions.	☐	☐

Unit 3 Travel and tourism

READING

QUESTION 1

Look at the five pictures of signs below. Someone asks you what each sign means. For each sign put a tick in one of the boxes – like this √ – to show the correct answer.

1.

☐ The sightseeing bus has left.

☐ The sightseeing bus stops here.

☐ The sightseeing bus is full.

☐ The sightseeing bus is late.

2.

☐ You can change money here.

☐ You should have the correct money.

☐ Please check if your change is right.

☐ Make sure you pay here.

≫→

3.

PARKING SPACE FOR STATION USERS ONLY

☐ You must pay to park here.

☐ If you use the train you can park here.

☐ This space is for railway officials.

☐ No one is allowed to park here.

4.

Passengers must be in possession of a ticket before travelling

☐ You can buy your ticket during the journey.

☐ You pay when you get off.

☐ You have to book a seat before travelling.

☐ You have to buy a ticket before your journey.

5.

Visas will only be issued to holders of return air tickets

☐ Get a visa before booking your flight.

☐ Book a return flight before you ask for a visa.

☐ You can't fly without a visa.

☐ Apply for a visa before you book your return flight.

QUESTION 2

Read the article below and circle the letter next to the word that best fits each space.

EXAMPLE: You can catch the 53 bus at the .... on the corner.

    A   board   (B)   stop   C   pole   D   sign

When you are driving abroad you should make sure that
you have all your documents with you. These
(1) .... your passport, your driving licence and
insurance papers. It (2) .... be very inconvenient if
you (3) .... any of these or if you cannot find
(4) .... quickly. You must also make sure that your
car has a nationality plate which shows the country
where the car is registered; for (5) ...., GB for
Great Britain, F for France, N for Norway and so on.
    In some (6) .... you have to pay if you don't
(7) .... motoring laws and this can sometimes cost
you a lot of money. For instance, you may have to pay
immediately if you are stopped by a police officer for
taking no notice of traffic lights, speed (8) .... or if
you allow children (9) .... the age of twelve to
(10) .... in the front seat of a vehicle.

1.	A include	B make	C mean	D contain
2.	A should	B can	C is	D has
3.	A miss	B hide	C lose	D pass
4.	A that	B those	C their	D them
5.	A once	B example	C general	D fact
6.	A countries	B positions	C ways	D routes
7.	A do	B allow	C obey	D continue
8.	A marks	B spots	C limits	D numbers
9.	A under	B lower	C over	D behind
10.	A follow	B pass	C travel	D wait

QUESTION 3

Look at these descriptions of camping grounds taken from a tourist guide book, then answer the questions.

(A) **Adleigh Woods Park**

Lovely surroundings in area of lakes and woods. Large camp with swimming pool, children's pool and playground. Camp cafe serves evening meals. Bookings Saturday to Saturday only.
phone 441 312326

(B) **Derston Gardens**

One of the few camps to be found in a town centre. Quiet and private. No pets allowed. Popular camp. Maximum 3 nights stay.
phone 441 213557

(C) **Grange Farm Camping Ground**

Large quiet camp set in woods and close to river. (Suitable for experienced swimmers only.) 4 tennis courts. No playground. Self-service restaurant. Kitchens available for campers to cook own meals. No animals.
phone 441 317859

(D) **Highcliff Camp**

Modern camping ground, popular with young people. Nightly discos and other entertainment included in price. Plenty of opportunities for water sports including sailing. No restaurant. Bookings weekend to weekend only.
phone 441 536565

(E) **Kingswater Beach Park**

Well-planned camp close to beach. TV room. Safe play area for small children. Excellent centre for touring. Frequent buses and trains to city centre.
phone 441 516435

(F) **Moorgate Park**

Large camping area 2 kms from town beside deep lake. (Dangerous for small children.) Good centre for fishing, sailing and waterskiing. Open-air countryside museum.
phone 441 319856

The people below are all going camping. Put a tick in the box to show the place you think is best for each group. More than one answer may be possible.

	A	B	C	D	E	F
1. Mr & Mrs Smith and their two young children will be travelling by train. They want to arrive on Wednesday and camp for three nights.	☐	☐	☐	☐	☐	☐
2. The Andertons and their grown-up children want somewhere they can do water sports. Their holiday will begin on Tuesday.	☐	☐	☐	☐	☐	☐
3. The Baxter family want to start their holiday this weekend and stay at a camp where they don't have to cook for themselves at night. The children want to learn to swim.	☐	☐	☐	☐	☐	☐
4. Jean and her friends have just left school and they want a camp where they can swim during the day and enjoy themselves in the evenings at no extra cost.	☐	☐	☐	☐	☐	☐
5. Mrs Eldon and her sister would like somewhere out of town where there won't be lots of children, and where she can take her dog.	☐	☐	☐	☐	☐	☐

QUESTION 4

Look at the 'Teen Travel Club' leaflet. If you agree with the statement, put a tick in the box under 'Yes'. If you do not agree, tick the box under 'No'.

		Yes	No
1.	Everyone over the age of 15 can join the Teen Travel Club.	☐	☐
2.	You need to take proof of your age to join the Club.	☐	☐
3.	You will need to have a photo of yourself.	☐	☐
4.	You do not have to pay to be a member.	☐	☐
5.	You give your ticket to the bus driver.	☐	☐
6.	There is no time limit on your ticket.	☐	☐
7.	Tickets can be bought at a shop.	☐	☐
8.	You need your membership card when you travel by bus.	☐	☐
9.	You can pay for a friend's fare by stamping your ticket.	☐	☐
10.	You can use Teen Travel tickets on any service.	☐	☐

TEEN
TRAVEL
CLUB

If you're aged 16, 17, 18 or 19 and would like to be able to afford to go out more often, why not join the Teen Travel Club and get cheaper bus travel.

To join all you have to do is to fill in a form and take it to your nearest bus station. You will also need to produce your birth certificate and a passport-sized photograph of yourself.

You will be given a free Teen Travel membership card which will allow you to travel at a reduced cost.

Once you're a member of the Teen Travel Club you can buy tickets at any bus station, post office or rail ticket office. Each ticket you buy is divided into 10 parts; when you get on the bus you put the ticket into a special machine which will then stamp one part.

The tickets last as long as you like and it doesn't matter how long it takes you to use up all the journeys. However, you must remember to take your membership card with you when you use your ticket otherwise you may have to pay the full fare if your ticket is checked.

Teen Travel tickets cannot be used by more than one person at a time nor can they be used on night services or the 709 express bus service.

Ten 23p Journeys	Fare Band 2	**£1.70**
Ten 30p Journeys	Fare Band 3	**£2.20**
Ten 35p Journeys	Fare Band 4	**£2.55**
Ten any distance Journeys		**£3.35**

QUESTION 5

Read the following passage and then answer the questions below. You must put a tick in the correct box or write in a few words.

* First, although it's not an absolute rule, we do seriously suggest you limit yourself to only one piece of hand luggage when you fly.
* We know you have probably a long list of good reasons for wanting to take as much baggage as possible with you inside the aircraft cabin – and we do try to help as much as we can.
* Our aim is to provide as much space as possible in the cabin for hand baggage. With this in mind, we have installed in the majority of our aircraft large cupboards above the seats, capable of taking most pieces of hand luggage. There is also, of course, the usual space for putting small cases under the seats.
* But we do have to be practical, and also remember the other passengers. We must also obey the safety rules – and that means hand baggage can only be put in the places described above during the flight.
* It is likely that you will be able to take two pieces of hand baggage with you, even if you are travelling tourist class, but when flights are heavily booked, or when your aircraft has limited space for hand baggage, we may need to ask you to limit the amount of cabin baggage.
* That is why we suggest you only take one piece of cabin baggage with you. It will avoid any possible difficulties when you check in for your flight.
* If you are flying on Concorde, in First Class or Super Club, you can take a suit carrier on board with you as well.
* And whichever class you are in you can also take duty free goods and small personal possessions like a handbag, camera, reading material etc.

1. This is from ☐ a tourist guide book.

    ☐ an insurance company handout.

    ☐ a government notice.

    ☐ an airline handout.

2. What is the writer doing? ☐ complaining about airline rules

    ☐ proposing changes to airline rules

    ☐ explaining airline rules

    ☐ complaining about other passengers

3. What do air safety rules say about hand baggage?

   ....

   ....

4. The main aim of the writer is to persuade the readers that they

   ....

   ....

5. Put a tick to show which of these passengers will have problems at check-in.

WRITING

QUESTION 6

Here are some sentences about things you should do at an airport. Finish the second sentence so that it has the same meaning as the first.

EXAMPLE: Many airports never close.

Many airports are *always opens.*

1. On arrival at the airport please go straight to the check-in desk.

    When ....

2. Remember to check your flight number.

    Don't ....

3. Your passport will be checked in the Immigration Hall.

    The Immigration officials ....

4. Tax free goods can be bought before you get on the plane.

    You ....

5. Some tax free goods will be on sale during your flight.

    There ....

QUESTION 7

You want advice from a travel agent about where to go on holiday. Use the form below to help you fill out the details of the kind of holiday you want. Use about 50 words.

HOLIDAY REQUEST FORM

Please help your travel agent by filling in this form as fully as you can

Which countries are you interested in?

Do you want a touring holiday?

Do you want to camp?

Which month do you want to go away?

How long will your holiday be?

Are you travelling alone/with family and friends?

Any special requests?

QUESTION 8

An English friend is going to visit your country for the first time. Write a letter to him/her giving all the information you think may be useful. Use the notes below to help you. Write about 100 words.

Transport – cheapest? best?
Shops – opening times
Banks –   "   "
Places to eat
Famous tourist sights

Dear.......................,

    I'm so pleased you're going to visit my country. You'll need to know about various things so I'll try to give you as much information as I can. First of all...

....

....

....

....

....

....

....

....

....

....

....

....

....

LISTENING

QUESTION 9

Put a tick in the box you think is the most suitable.

EXAMPLE:

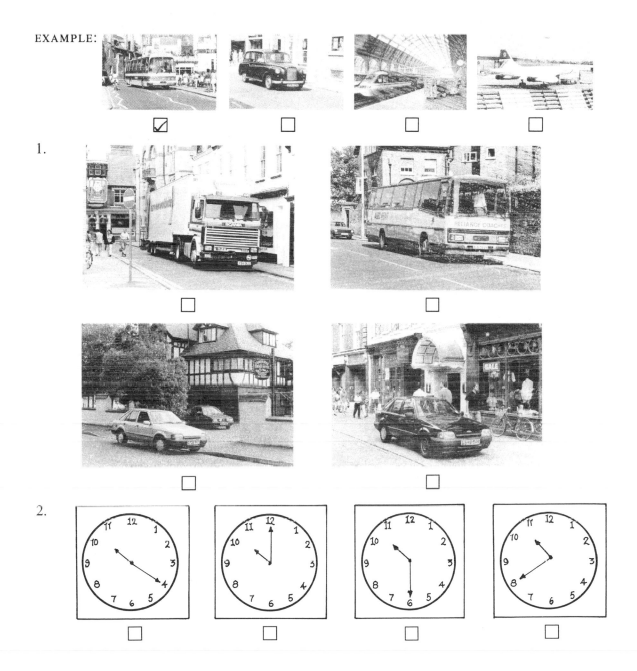

3.

☐

☐

☐

☐

4.

☐

☐

☐

☐

5.

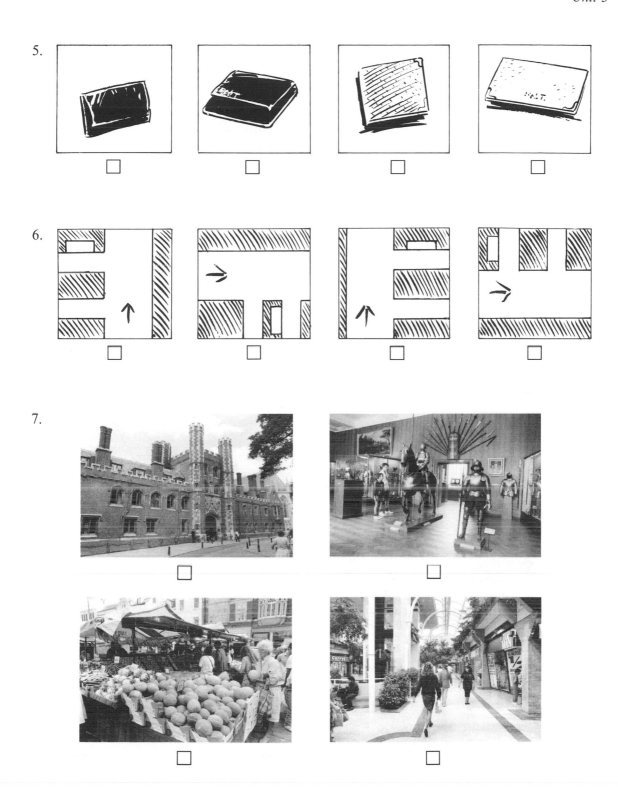

6.

7.

QUESTION 10

Listen to these flight announcements. Put a tick in the box you think is the most suitable.

1. Flight number YZ 243 is going to Ankara. ☐
   Anchorage. ☐
   Accra. ☐
   Dakar. ☐

2. Dominic Andrews is a pilot. ☐
   a passenger. ☐
   on the security staff. ☐
   on the airline staff. ☐

3. For the flight to New York go to Gate   9. ☐
   16. ☐
   19. ☐
   90. ☐

4. The flight to Jakarta is early. ☐
   on time. ☐
   cancelled. ☐
   late. ☐

5. Mr and Mrs El Ghazi will find Mustapha on the aeroplane. ☐
   at Gate 21. ☐
   in the arrivals hall. ☐
   at the Customs desk. ☐

6. The flight from Cairo is late because of freezing fog. ☐
   snow and ice. ☐
   low cloud. ☐
   heavy rain. ☐

QUESTION 11

Fill in the gaps with the information needed and put a tick in the box you think is the most suitable.

The castle closes at (1) ....

For a tour of the castle, go to the (2) ....
    at 11 a.m.

The show called "Local Artists" has pictures
    by (3)..........................

(4) Anderson's Hall has a show of
- ☐ drawings.
- ☐ paintings.
- ☐ photographs.
- ☐ models.

The silver and glass can be seen on (5)....................
    and .... afternoons.

(6) You can listen to Indian music
- ☐ in the open air.
- ☐ in a tent.
- ☐ in a concert hall.
- ☐ in a restaurant.

QUESTION 12

If you agree with the statement, put a tick in the box under 'Yes'. If you do not agree, put a tick under 'No'.

		Yes	No
1.	The girl asks to go to Ivy Bank Gardens.	☐	☐
2.	The taxi driver thinks hotels are very expensive.	☐	☐
3.	The girl disagrees with the driver's opinion of hotels.	☐	☐
4.	The girl has given the wrong address.	☐	☐
5.	The driver is happy to continue the journey.	☐	☐

Unit 4   Family, education and society

READING

QUESTION 1

Look at the five pictures of signs below. Someone asks you what each sign means. For each sign put a tick in one of the boxes – like this √ – to show the correct answer.

1.

☐ Patel wants you to choose him on Thursday.

☐ Patel will win this Thursday.

☐ Patel wants you to ring him about Thursday.

☐ Patel wants you to meet him on Thursday.

2.

☐ Professor Gilroy is teaching all day.

☐ Professor Gilroy will be late.

☐ Professor Gilroy has a new class.

☐ Professor Gilroy is not teaching today.

⟫→

3.

☐ Family tickets save time.

☐ Family tickets save money.

☐ Family tickets may be more expensive.

☐ Family tickets have gone down in price.

4.

☐ Many people don't want a motorway.

☐ Building the motorway starts today.

☐ People are going to talk about building a motorway.

☐ Everyone travelling on the motorway should meet here.

5.

☐ You have forgotten to make a phonecall.

☐ Why not make a phonecall?

☐ Phonecalls are cheaper now.

☐ You have lost a phone number.

QUESTION 2

Read the article below and circle the letter next to the word that best fits each space.

EXAMPLE: In the UK the .... number of children in a family is two.

    A   ordinary   B   common   C   usual   (D)   average

"My home is in the air – I do an enormous amount of travelling. It is a fast life and (1) .... of work, but I like it and that is the only way (2) .... me. Everything is tiring – music, travelling – but what can I do? I am not (3) .... to complaining. It is hard to imagine now (4) .... I will ever be very long in one place. My home town is on the Caspian Sea. There is sea, wind, sun and (5) .... many tourists and hotels. I have my own flat with four or five rooms, but I am seldom there. If I am there for a day or two I prefer to (6) .... with my mother and grandmother. They live in a small house, (7) .... it is very comfortable and my mother cooks for me. I like good, simple food.

I have no wife, no brothers or sisters and my father (8) .... when I was seven. He was an engineer and I don't (9) .... him very well. He liked music very much and wanted me to (10) .... a musician."

1.	A	most	B	full	C	complete	D	more
2.	A	for	B	to	C	in	D	by
3.	A	wanted	B	taken	C	used	D	known
4.	A	and	B	so	C	while	D	that
5.	A	far	B	too	C	much	D	more
6.	A	stay	B	go	C	do	D	spend
7.	A	but	B	since	C	even	D	which
8.	A	killed	B	gone	C	passed	D	died
9.	A	know	B	remember	C	remind	D	see
10.	A	become	B	turn	C	develop	D	grow

QUESTION 3

Look at this school report for Sarah Targett, then answer the questions.

LAMPTON SCHOOL   TERM REPORT

Name SARAH TARGETT

Class 3B

Age 13

Mathematics

Sometimes very good, but often spoilt because she is careless about finishing her homework. She really must try to hand in her work at the right time!

J.N

English

She has worked hard throughout the term. She shows a good understanding of what she reads. She often has problems with written work as she doesn't take enough time to organize her ideas before starting to write. Her handwriting is neat but she can be rather slow.

E.F.

Science

Sarah is getting on well. She is neat and remembers facts well.

MM

History

She has made good progress during the term and handed in an excellent piece of work on English Kings and Queens. She sometimes has difficulty remembering dates and needs to put in more time on this at home.   LR

Geography

Sarah enjoys this subject and she has produced some very good work this term. She still needs to take care when she is drawing maps, although they are much tidier than they used to be.

MM

Music

Sarah is doing very well; she has a pleasant voice and she comes to practices regularly E.B.

Sport

Good. She's got lots of energy and has been a very active member of the girls' football team. She's also learnt to swim at last.   A.T.

Class teacher's report

Sarah is a very pleasant and helpful member of class. There are certain subjects, especially Maths, where she needs to make more effort, but on the whole she is working well.   MM

Date 8/12/91   **Signed** Sheila King   **Head Teacher**

Visual material for the Oral

1A

1B

1C

2A

2B

2C

3A

SOUTH OF ENGLAND ONE DAY TOUR

DEPART LONDON 7.30 a.m.
First stop: *Salisbury*

Second stop: *lunch at country hotel in New Forest (one of England's oldest National Parks)*

Third stop: *Bournemouth for shopping (or just relax by the sea)*

RETURN LONDON 7.30 p.m.
£12.00 including lunch

3B

3C

4A

student numbers?
cost?
times of classes?
conversation only?
special interest lessons?

4B

WESSEX LANGUAGE SCHOOL

Small classes — maximum 10 per class

19.30 — 21.00 Mon, Tues, Wed, Thurs

English for Scientists 18.00 — 19.00 Tues & Wed

Phone 82 8340

We're not the cheapest — but we are the best!

4C

4D

5A

5B

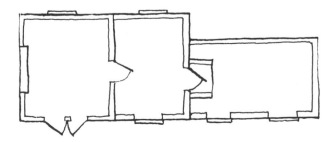

If you think a statement is true, put a tick in the box under 'Yes'. If not, tick the box under 'No'.

		Yes	No
1.	Sarah sometimes forgets to give in her mathematics homework.	☐	☐
2.	She has problems with reading.	☐	☐
3.	Her handwriting is unclear.	☐	☐
4.	She finds it difficult to plan her English written work.	☐	☐
5.	Sarah's mapwork is becoming more untidy.	☐	☐
6.	In history she needs to be more careful with her written work.	☐	☐
7.	She sings well.	☐	☐
8.	She has only just learnt to swim.	☐	☐
9.	Her class teacher wishes Sarah would behave better.	☐	☐
10.	She is a lazy pupil.	☐	☐

QUESTION 4

Look at the page from a local newspaper on page 60. It shows six advertisements from organisations asking for help in different ways. Below is a list of things they ask for. Write the letter A, B, C, D, E or F in the box next to the sentence which you think fits best.

1. ☐ want people to help paint some rooms
2. ☐ need money to pay nurses
3. ☐ want paint to use themselves
4. ☐ need money to pay rent
5. ☐ need money for cooking equipment
6. ☐ want families to invite children for visits

A TIME FOR GIVING

This is a time of year when we think about giving and receiving presents. For organisations which work with the less fortunate members of our society, it can be a difficult time.

Can YOU find a little extra to give? On this page we suggest a few local organisations you might like to help.

Ⓐ Littleton Children's Home

We DON'T want your money, but children's toys, books and clothes IN GOOD CONDITION would be very welcome.

Also – we are looking for friendly families who would take our children into their homes for a few hours or days as guests. You have so much – will you share it?

Phone Sister Thomas on 55671

Ⓑ Littleton Children's Hospice

We look after a small number of very sick children. This important work needs skill and love. We cannot continue without gifts of money to pay for more nursing staff. We also need story books and toys suitable for quiet games.

Please contact The Secretary, Littleton Children's Hospice, Newby Road.

Ⓒ *Rosemary Rest Home*   *tel. 21243*

Our old people would love to see you – could you spare an hour or two each week to visit an old lady or gentleman and help them to keep in touch with the modern world? Or perhaps you would prefer to help make the home look a bit more cheerful? We need strong, active people to help paint our sitting-rooms. We've got the materials – have you got the time?

Ⓓ Street Food

In the winter weather, it's no fun being homeless. It's even worse if you're hungry. We give hot food to at least fifty people every night. It's hard work, but very necessary. Can you come and help? If not, can you find a little money? We use a very old kitchen, and we urgently need some new saucepans. Money for new ones would be most welcome indeed.

Contact Street Food, c/o Mary's House, Elming Way. Phone 27713

Ⓔ Littleton Youth Club

Have you got an unwanted chair? – record-player? – pot of paint?

Because we can use them!

We want to get to work on our meeting room!

Please phone 66231 and we'll be happy to collect anything you can give us.

Thank you!

Ⓕ The Night Shelter

We offer a warm bed for the night to anyone who has nowhere to go. We rent the former Commercial Hotel on Greene Street. Although it is not expensive, we never seem to have quite enough money. Can you let us have a few pounds? Any amount, however small, will be such a help.

Send it to us at 15, Greene St., Littleton. Please make cheques payable to Night Shelter.

QUESTION 5

Read this passage and then answer the questions below. You must put a tick in the correct box or write in a few words.

I am often asked whether we will do anything about the taxes we all have to pay. Of course, what people mean is that they don't want to pay so much. But I have to ask in return which services they would like to lose. For we cannot expect to have modern hospitals, well-kept roads, good schools or attractive parks if we are not prepared to pay for these things. Our children do not think that schools and colleges are only for the sons and daughters of the rich, as once they were. More and more of us are living longer and longer. We all feel that we should be able to see a doctor when we need to. Old people should not suffer because they are afraid of the doctor's bill. In our society, we are proud of the fact that no one is asked whether they can pay the bill before they are allowed into a hospital. But if we want to continue to provide for all the needs of our society, we must remember that nothing in life is free. My party does not promise to cut taxes immediately. But we do promise to continue all the services that our taxes pay for, and we hope that we will manage things so well that after a short time some taxes may be reduced.

1. This is from ☐ a teacher's diary.

    ☐ a personal letter.

    ☐ a political message.

    ☐ a medical book.

2. What is the writer's intention? ☐ to explain his ideas

    ☐ to describe the past

    ☐ to warn about money problems

    ☐ to ask for advice

3. The writer thinks people who complain about taxes should

    ....

    ....

4. What is the attitude of modern children towards education?

    ....

    ....

5. One of these people shares the same ideas as the writer. Put a tick in the box under the one you think it is.

A

THE TROUBLE WITH PEOPLE NOWADAYS IS THAT THEY ALL WANT SOMETHING FOR NOTHING. THEY THINK THEY SHOULD BE ABLE TO GET WHATEVER THEY WANT, BUT THEY DON'T REALISE THAT SOME ONE IS GOING TO HAVE TO PAY FOR IT IN THE END !

☐

B

I JUST DON'T KNOW WHERE I'M GOING TO FIND THE MONEY I NEED. THERE'S SO MUCH TO PAY FOR – THE CHILDREN'S SCHOOL, THE DOCTOR, THE GROCERY BILL AND MY TAX ! WHAT AM I GOING TO DO ?

☐

C

I KNOW I OUGHT TO GO AND SEE THE DOCTOR, BUT I DON'T THINK I CAN AFFORD IT. I KNOW HE'LL TELL ME TO BUY SOME MEDICINE, BUT I JUST HAVEN'T GOT THE MONEY.

☐

D

OF COURSE, WHAT THE GOVERNMENT OUGHT TO DO IS GIVE PEOPLE CONTROL OF THEIR OWN MONEY. IF WE DIDN'T HAVE TO PAY TAXES, WE'D BE ABLE TO AFFORD TO PAY ALL OUR OWN BILLS. WE WOULDN'T NEED FREE SCHOOLS AND HOSPITALS.

☐

WRITING

QUESTION 6

Here are some sentences about the English education system. Finish the second sentence so that it has the same meaning as the first.

EXAMPLE: You do not have to pay for secondary education in Britain.

Secondary education *is free in Britain.*

1. Children cannot start school until they are five years old.

   Children are ....

2. The number of children in a primary school is usually quite small.

   A primary school ....

3. Secondary schools are much bigger than primary schools.

   Primary schools..

4. Most secondary schools are for boys and girls.

   Nearly ....

5. The system has both private and state schools.

   There ....

QUESTION 7

You are going to take part in an exchange programme with a British family. You will stay with the family in Britain for two weeks and a British student will stay with you for another two weeks. Fill in the form below so that your details can be matched with your exchange family's details.

FIRST NAME ....

SURNAME ....

ADDRESS ....

....

DATE OF BIRTH ....

NATIONALITY ....

HAVE YOU ANY BROTHERS OR SISTERS? ....

WHICH MONTH WOULD YOU LIKE TO VISIT BRITAIN? ....

HAVE YOU BEEN TO BRITAIN BEFORE? ....

IF YES, WHERE AND FOR HOW LONG? ....

....

WHAT ARE YOUR HOBBIES/INTERESTS? ....

....

....

DO YOU SMOKE? ....

ANY SPECIAL REQUESTS? (eg food, medical care, own room, etc)

....

....

WHY DO YOU WANT TO COME TO BRITAIN? ....

....

....

QUESTION 8

You are attending a language school in the UK. Below is your timetable. Write a letter to a friend telling him/her about your life here. Write about 100 words.

	MONDAY	**TUESDAY**	**WEDNESDAY**	**THURSDAY**	**FRIDAY**
am	SPEAKING	LIBRARY	LISTENING	READING	WRITING
	WRITING	VISIT	SPEAKING	SPEAKING	LISTENING
	L	U	N	C	H
pm	LANGUAGE THROUGH SONGS	WORD GAMES	SPORTS AFTERNOON	MUSEUM VISIT	SPECIAL INTEREST CLASSES
	Students MUST attend all morning classes.				
	Afternoon classes and evening meetings (eg film club, music society, cookery class) are open to all those who wish to attend.				

Dear ....,

I arrived safely and have already started at language school. It's hard work, but quite interesting...

....

....

....

....

....

....

LISTENING

QUESTION 9

Put a tick in the box you think is the most suitable.

EXAMPLE:

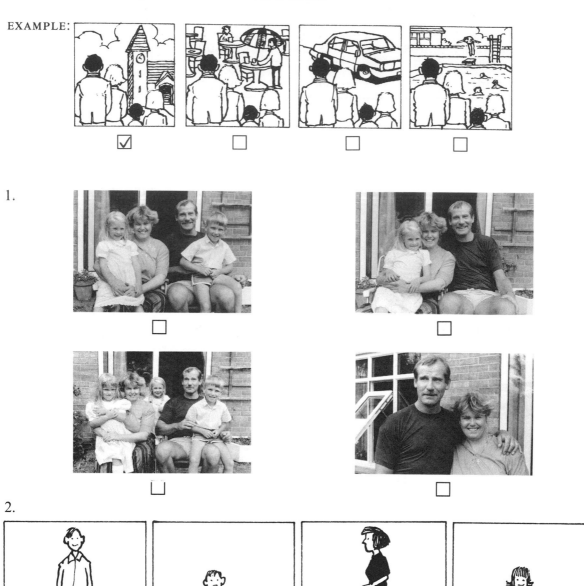

1.

2.

3.

□　　　　□　　　　□　　　　□

4.

□　　　　□　　　　□　　　　□

5.

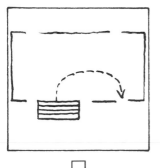 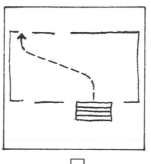 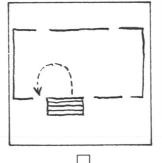 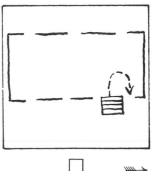

□　　　　□　　　　□　　　　□　　≫→

6.

☐

☐

☐

☐

7.

☐

☐

☐

☐

QUESTION 10

Listen to Mr Brook, the head of a language school, then put a tick in the box you think is the most suitable.

① To join a special interest class, the students have to
      speak to Mr Brook. ☐
      go to Room 45. ☐
      write their name on a list. ☐
      fill in a form. ☐

② Philip's class is on speaking. ☐
                  listening. ☐
                  science. ☐
                  music. ☐

③ Alison will talk about sport. ☐
                     films. ☐
                     places in Britain. ☐
                     books. ☐

④ Mike's going to explain old English songs. ☐
                       English music. ☐
                       modern songs. ☐
                       his own songs. ☐

⑤ Nicky's class is for the top class only. ☐
                  literature students only. ☐
                  any student. ☐
                  exam students only. ☐

⑥ Mr Brook's class is about science. ☐
                     mathematics. ☐
                     how to pronounce English. ☐
                     life in Britain. ☐

QUESTION 11

Write in the information needed below.

MEETING AT TOWN HALL

1st speaker – Mrs Bradley:
   More money for hospital &
   children's play (1) ....
Bus service must be (2) ....
Continue travel for (3)..................
                              over 65.

2nd speaker – Mr Bennett :
New swimming pool and (4)..................
Car parks will end traffic
jams in (5)............... ....
New street lamps needed
in (6)............ ....

3rd speaker Mrs J...

QUESTION 12

If you agree with the statement, put a tick in the box under 'Yes'. If you do not agree, put a tick under 'No'.

	Yes	No
1. The girl wants to go to France with her friends.	☐	☐
2. The girl's mother thinks the holiday is a good idea.	☐	☐
3. The girl's father refuses to listen to her suggestion.	☐	☐
4. The girl says she can pay for the holiday herself.	☐	☐
5. The girl's father gets very angry with her.	☐	☐

Unit 5   PET practice test paper

READING

QUESTION 1

Look at the five pictures of signs below. Someone asks you what each sign means. For each sign put a tick in one of the boxes   like this √ – to show the correct answer.

1.

☐ The business has closed down.

☐ The business has a new address.

☐ The business has been sold.

☐ The business has changed owners.

2.

☐ Open the window carefully.

☐ This window cannot be opened.

☐ Do not put anything against the window.

☐ Do not put your head out of the window.

⋙→

3.

☐ Use the other door.

☐ Don't lock this door.

☐ Wait here until the door is opened.

☐ Don't leave this door open.

4.

☐ The college has moved to a new building.

☐ If you move house, tell the College Office.

☐ Tell the College Office your home address when you first arrive.

☐ Ask at the College Office if you want to change your room.

5.

☐ If your guests break anything, you'll have to pay.

☐ If guests are hurt, members have to look after them.

☐ Please don't let guests make too much noise.

☐ Please remember to look after guests very politely.

QUESTION 2

Read the article below and circle the letter next to the word that best fits each space.

EXAMPLE: I hate travelling .... air.

    A on   B in   C through   Ⓓ by

> For many people, travelling by plane is an exciting experience. Others, however, find the whole idea quite terrifying, (1) .... flying is no more dangerous (2) .... any other form of travel and some experts say it is considerably safer. It is known, however, that most accidents occur (3) .... take-off and landing when a (4) .... decisions are vitally important.
>
> The people (5) .... job it is to look (6) .... the passengers – the stewards and stewardesses – play an important part in helping passengers to (7) .... safe and comfortable. Indeed for many passengers being (8) .... such care of is all part of the total experience. (9) .... other form of travel involves waiting on people in quite the same (10) ...., with food, drink, newspapers, magazines, music and even video films.

1. A although   B too   C and   D because

2. A than   B as   C then   D with

3. A while   B during   C for   D through

4. A leader's   B chief's   C driver's   D pilot's

5. A whose   B which   C their   D that

6. A for   B up   C after   D round

7. A feel   B rest   C experience   D lie

8. A given   B kept   C shown   D taken

9. A Any   B No   C All   D Not

10. A way   B kind   C sort   D part

QUESTION 3

Below is a list of West Country attractions. Read the details and then answer the questions.

country museum

The museum of the Somerset countryside housed in an old farm close to the world famous Glastonbury Abbey. Permanent displays include the farm kitchen and dairy. Small shop selling postcards and home-grown vegetables.

emsley gardens

Hundreds of colourful birds in lovely natural surroundings. Large areas of woodland, rose gardens and lakes. During the summer months there is a Pets' Corner, organised walks for children, and outdoor art displays.

westbury park

Open all year; 80 acres of ancient forest dating back over thousands of years. The grounds have changed very little since the eleventh century when the first owner bought the land. Many different varieties of trees and plants in wild surroundings. No restaurant, but picnic area in the grounds.

rivel zoo

One of the most famous zoos in the West Country with some of the best designed cages and viewing platforms in the world. Regular feeding times for most animals throughout the day and children encouraged to take part under direction of zoo keepers. Cafe open all day as well as picnic areas.

shelton house

A thirteenth century manor house once part of a medieval village. People have lived in this house for over 700 years. Inside are many valuable pictures and objects; outside, beautiful gardens with rare plants and flowers. Coffee shop open in afternoons only.

The five people below want to visit the West Country. Put a tick in the box to show the place you think is best for each person.

	Country Museum	Westbury Park	Shelton House	Emsley Gardens	Rivel Zoo
1. Mrs Tondo doesn't mind where she spends the morning so long as she can have a quick lunch there before going on to the theatre in the afternoon.	☐	☐	☐	☐	☐
2. Mr Khalid is interested in art but doesn't like wandering around in the open air as he finds the climate very cold.	☐	☐	☐	☐	☐
3. Mr Tuv likes taking photographs of flowers and would like to spend a few hours alone without having to look afer his eight-year-old daughter.	☐	☐	☐	☐	☐
4. Miss Delacroix is an artist who earns her living by painting countryside scenes and especially areas where nature has not been disturbed.	☐	☐	☐	☐	☐
5. Miss Landolt is interested in old buildings particularly if they are in their original state as family homes and not turned into display centres.	☐	☐	☐	☐	☐

QUESTION 4

Look at this page of newspaper advertisements and write the telephone number each of these people needs to ring to get more information.

1 I need to get to work late at night.

....

2 I must have my car cleaned regularly.

....

3 My wife died last year. I want to sell my house and live in a home where I can feel safe and have people of my own age to talk to.

....

4 My school running team want shirts with the name of our school on them.

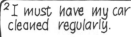

....

5 I need to have some really smart clothes made. Something I can wear to business meetings.

....

6 I've got to get some cleaners organised for the offices and workshops.

....

7 I need a new desk.

....

8 I want to organise an educational trip for my class of ten-year olds. A local company would be best.

....

9 I'm going to a very fashionable party but I can't afford to buy an evening dress!

....

10 We're giving a club party- I've got to find some really exciting lighting for the disco.

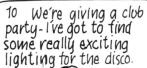

....

YORK CLEANING SERVICES

ALL ASPECTS OF INDUSTRIAL
AND
COMMERCIAL CLEANING

Daytime: (0783) 7892
Evenings: (0783) 6042/6207

YORK STAGE SERVICES

*FOR YOUR PROFESSIONAL &
AMATEUR PRODUCTIONS
PARTIES & DANCES*
Theatrical and disco lighting, stage make-up,
wigs, fancy dress, ballet and dance wear.
11 ST. GEORGES ST., YORK.
TEL: YORK (0780) 5453
Postal enquiries welcome

EVERYTHING FOR THE CAKE DECORATOR

Tins, Drums, Books, Ornaments,
Turntables, Bekernal tubes, Regalica,
White almond paste, Meriwhite Cake
boxes, Colours, Ribbons
and lots more.

TINS AND CAKE STANDS FOR HIRE

TUITION IN SUGARCRAFT
Mon.–Thu 9.30–12 & 1–3.30

**ROMNEY ICING CENTRE
69 Manor Way, Romney.
Tel: Romney (0778) 34790**

Wedding Hire

Outfits for brides/grooms and attendants
as well as a selection of ladies hats. Also
available cakes and stationery all at
economical rates.
Our Day
Telephone: (0480) 21429

CAR VALETER

High standard private and business
car and van valeting

FOR APPOINTMENT CONTACT
ROUNDABOUT AUTOCLEAN
Nikki or Phil Gaynes
(0783) 7860 anytime

FANCY DRESS HIRE
CARNIVALS, FETES & PARTIES
All costumes are washed or dry-cleaned after
every hire.

CLOTHESLINE

Call in at:
27 Evelyn Road, Cambridge
or phone Cambridge (0223) 21330

"*I have the simplest tastes, I am always
satisfied with the best*".
OSCAR WILDE

*In other words, if you are serious
about hi-fi, then come to the one
place where the range of products
is an enthusiast's vocabulary.*

WENSLEY
AUDIO
SYSTEMS

Simply better hi-fi

489 Lincoln Road, York.
Telephone (0733) 55883

FARRE TRAVEL

Local, contracts, long distance functions.
Concessions for OAP's & disabled.
Single fare at all times.
Genuine 24 hour service

**PETERBOROUGH
(0733) 6945**
28 Farre Road, Peterborough

YOU SHALL GO TO THE BALL

With a dress hired from Susanna's
Ballgowns, evening and cocktail dresses for hire.
Menswear hire also available now.
Phone any time for an appointment.
Susanna's
Mortlock Street, Romney. Tel: Romney (0763) 6198

**REST
HAVEN**

Station Road,
Pitton,
Cambridgeshire
Tel: (0358) 72091

Registered Private Home for the Elderly
A warm, caring and friendly home in a relaxed
environment, providing qualified staff. A varied
menu, special diets, lift, single & shared rooms with
wash hand basin, and call system as standard.
Proprietor: L.S. Roberts

SUITS for the CONNOISSEUR
Handmade personally by
Ex-Saville Row Tailor,
From £165
Ladies' and Gentlemen's Tailoring to
exceptionally high standards
ALTERATIONS
PAUL D. TABACEK
10 Field Road, Grimsby. Tel: Grimsby 81363

GRANVILLE CATERING

*Complete Outside Catering Service
We take very special care of you*

**Head Office: Hatcher's Farm, Farley.
Telephone:
Huntingdon (0480) 7208**

SHELVES & SPACES FURNITURE

High Class Wooden Furniture for Homes, Offices,
Hotels, Shop and Exhibition Displays

*DESIGNED AND
MANUFACTURED TO ORDER*

Contact
SHELVES & SPACES FURNITURE
on Peterborough 32028 (24 hr answer service)

TELL-ME-T

T-Shirts – Sweat Shirts
Promotional Items
Printed to your requirements
Printed up to 4 colours
Design service available
5, Oscar Drive, Henfield
Tel: (0223) 41107

VISIT THE 'NEWS'

**Have you ever wanted to see your
local newspaper being produced?**

Well now you can.

Tours of the 'News' offices in Pitton
are now available for groups of
'News' readers.

To find out more telephone Lucy Lock,
Promotions Department.
Tel. Pitton 35887

Pitton Newspapers

Publishers of
the 'Pitton News' & 'Weekly News' Series.

QUESTION 5

Read this passage and then answer the questions below. You must put a tick in the correct box or write a few words.

> . . . so that wasn't any good, either. However, I must tell you one rather good thing that's happened: we've got a new car at last! The children love it, because the back seat's nice and wide so they're not all crowded in, half on top of one another, kicking each other's legs and fighting. With luck, from now on, I should be able to drive to town and back without one of them being in tears for the whole journey. And what about the dog? Well there's a space for him behind the children, it's one of those cars with a fifth door at the back and an enormous space for dog, suitcases, shopping and so on. No doubt in the case of this family, it will be nasty objects like smelly football boots, but at least I'll be able to keep the front part a bit tidier than in the old car. Although I sometimes complain about Jim as a husband, I must say he's really been very generous about this car, because it wasn't cheap to buy, and it does use more petrol than some similar models. Enough about boring old cars – how are you and your family? Have you decided . . .

1. This is part of ☐ a letter to a friend.

   ☐ a letter to a newspaper.

   ☐ a magazine article.

   ☐ an advertisement.

2. What is the writer's aim? ☐ to encourage

   ☐ to worry

   ☐ to inform

   ☐ to persuade

3. What was the problem with the old car?

   ....

   ....

4. The main disadvantage of the new car is

    ....

    ....

5. Show which of these advertisements you think is for the car described here by circling the letter A, B, C or D.

A

B

C

D

WRITING

QUESTION 6

Here are some sentences about climate. Finish the second sentence so that it has the same meaning as the first.

EXAMPLE: It was the coldest winter they had ever had.

They had *never had a colder winter*.

1. Weather conditions influence most people's lives.

    Most people's lives are ....

2. Sunny weather can always be depended on in southern countries.

    People can always ....

3. There's usually plenty of sunshine in southern countries.

    It's usually ....

4. In countries like Britain the weather changes all the time.

    In countries like Britain the weather is very ....

5. Some visitors to Britain find the weather very depressing.

    Some visitors to Britain get ....

QUESTION 7

You want to join a sports club. Fill in the form below giving as much information as you can. Use about 50 words.

CITY *SPORTS CLUB*

Name ....

Which sport(s), if any, do you already play? ....

....

....

Which sport(s) do you want to play with the Club? ....

....

....

Are you interested in taking part in competitions? ....

Please give reasons for your answer ....

....

....

....

....

How did you hear about the City Sports Club? ....

....

....

....

SIGNATURE ....

QUESTION 8

You want to study at a language school in Britain. Write a letter to the Principal. Ask for details of courses, cost, accommodation and any other information you need to know. Tell her something about yourself. The letter has been started for you. Write about 100 words.

The Principal,
Wells Language School,
Somerset.

Dear Ms. Hibbens,

   I am writing to enquire about

....

....

....

....

....

....

....

....

....

....

....

....

....

....

....

....

LISTENING

QUESTION 9

Put a tick in the box you think is the most suitable.

EXAMPLE:

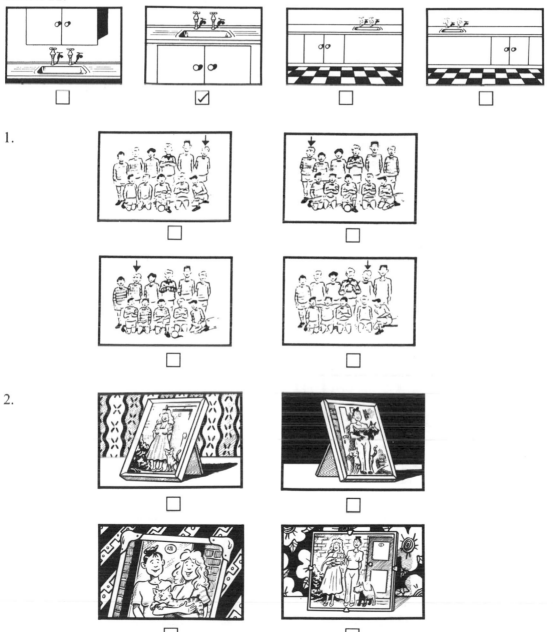

1.

2.

3.

☐

☐

☐

☐

4.

☐ ☐ ☐ ☐

5.

☐

☐

☐

☐

6.

☐

☐

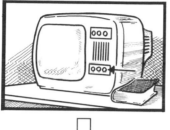

☐

☐

7.

☐

☐

☐

☐

QUESTION 10

In these notes put a tick in the box you think is the most suitable.

1. The tourists are sitting in a bus. ☐
   train. ☐
   boat. ☐
   coach. ☐

2. The first sight they see is the palace. ☐
   park. ☐
   wooden house. ☐
   canal. ☐

3. The wooden house was built by the king. ☐
   the council. ☐
   one of the Jacobsens. ☐
   a rich merchant. ☐

4. The summer house is now a family house. ☐
   restaurant. ☐
   museum. ☐
   royal apartment. ☐

5. The church was bombed. ☐
   burnt down. ☐
   flooded. ☐
   attacked. ☐

6. The Old Fish Market is now empty. ☐
   in ruins. ☐
   a meat market. ☐
   a flower market. ☐

QUESTION 11

Write in the information needed below.

```
NEWS REPORT


1 Serious fire on train which left Bristol at

  . . . . . . . . . . . . .

2 Both drivers . . . . . . . . . . . .

3 Trains still . . . . . . . . . . . .

4 Storms overnight on . . . . . . . . . . . . coast

5 Crops damaged and . . . . . . . . . . . . drowned

6 International Road Race begins at . . . . . . . . . . . .

  o'clock

7 At least . . . . . . . . . . . . people have entered
```

QUESTION 12

If you agree with the statement, put a tick in the box under 'Yes'. If you do not agree, put a tick under 'No'.

	Yes	No
1. The girl is cross because the boy is late.	☐	☐
2. The boy says the bus journey took 2 hours.	☐	☐
3. The girl has already eaten.	☐	☐
4. The boy knew the girl liked Robert's music.	☐	☐
5. The girl was planning to collect the cassettes later.	☐	☐